Full Circle

HOW TO LIVE, LOVE & LAUGH

EDNA NELSON

Copyright and Credits © 2021 Edna Nelson
ISBN: 978-1-991218-93-3 (Print)
Illustrator: Motsanaphe Morare (MoMaLifeLiving.com)
Editor and Proof-reader: Luyanda Thela
(ldlamini@thegoldengooseinstitute.com)

All rights reserved.
No part of this publication may be reproduced in any form or by any electronic or mechanical means, including information storage and retrieval systems, without permission in writing from the author, except by a reviewer who may quote brief passages in a review.

I would love to hear from you. Your questions, your comments are welcome. Don't be a stranger. My contact information is listed below, and I encourage you to contact me. I am also available for speaking engagements.

My email address is Email: ednanelson605@gmail.com

This book was published by
The Golden Goose Institute (Pty) Ltd

For further information email:
info@thegoldengooseinstitute.com

DEDICATION

To all who are seeking to live, laugh and love – may you do all three in this lifetime and to the fullest degree.

ACKNOWLEDGEMENTS

To Hugh Jackson, this book ensures that your story will never be forgotten.

To Lucas Philomon Nelson. Dad, you will always remain the most impressive man I know. Thank you for the values you taught me, the unconditional love you bestowed upon me and the beautiful memories you have left me with.

FOREWORD

Genuine. That is what our friendship is. Such a friendship can only be experienced with a person that can be described in the same manner: genuine. That's exactly what Edna is. My describing her using a word that is normally reserved for precious metals and stones is no coincidence. Just like these precious materials, she had to go through the fire, the grind, and the dust to shine in the end. During our twenty-nine-year friendship—which has rightfully graduated into a sisterhood by now—I have learned that there is no beating around the bush with her, there is no bush at all. If straight-talking was an Olympic sport, guess who would have a gold medal?

Having just suffered an incredible tragedy, you would think that Edna would not even be able to stand on her two feet, let alone step up to a podium and speak with such raw emotion that no eye was left dry. She did not stop there though, she also announced that she will be writing a book. This act of bravery reveals to us the strength of her character and personality. It is traits like these that you will experience as you embark on this journey with her. A journey where every word and every punctuation mark which is read will also automatically be felt deep in your soul.

Let us step into a genuine 360-degree experience where we will "live, love and laugh" together.

Kirschna Linden

REVIEWS

Life can throw some nasty surprises but it's how we react to these that truly enlightens us. Edna has shown resilience in her life and most importantly, given credit where credit is due— God. It takes a strong woman to stand up and still give God so much praise.

It was such a good and easy read. It is a book that not only gives hope but shows strength. A journey of hurt is never easy but this book shows that it can be overcome. Unconditional love will always prevail.

Alicia Stols
—*Proud mum. Writer. MA NWU VTC.*

A poignant story of love, insurmountable grief, and the intensity of healing. Edna has met with some of the harshest realities, however, how she has intentionally realigned herself with laughter, love, and life is a commendable way which we can all learn from to feel whole again... Coming Full Circle.

Lungile Ndlovu
—*Educator Extraordinaire*

CONTENTS

Dedication	3
Acknowledgements	5
Foreword	7
Reviews	9
Introduction	13
Chapter 1: The Happiness	17
Chapter 2: The Love	35
Chapter 3: The Hurt	47
Chapter 4: The Fear	71
Chapter 5: The Anger	81
Chapter 6: The Disbelief	87
Chapter 7: The Trauma	93
Chapter 8: The Healing	99
About the Author	109
References	115

INTRODUCTION

Young girls can start planning their wedding in their heads as early as when they are six years old. They pick out a career path to follow and figure out how many children to have. They believe that it would all work according to plan. Unfortunately, things do not always work out the way we had planned. When the plan does not work as predicted, it feels like we have failed.

I think the idea is placed in our minds because of the movies and fairy tales that we watch with our friends and family. At school, the teacher always asks what we would like to be when we grow up. We often look at how things are at home before we answer that question. We look at our parents and realise that that is how our lives are meant to be. We are supposed to get married, have children, have a good job and live life as a happy family. But does it always work out that way?

I met the man of my dreams, and my dreams became a reality. We fell in love and started planning our wedding and were searching for the perfect home to start our family. It was the best time of our lives. Everything was exactly how we wanted it to be. Until our lives came crumbling down.

I will be sharing my story on how my dreams came true and how easy it was for things to take a drastic turn. I take you on a journey of how to overcome the trauma of losing a loved one. Grief is not an easy aspect of life to deal with, but I will let you in on how I coped with it and how I wished I had handled things.

Who said life should be perfect? Does perfect only mean that you should have the perfect career, the perfect partner, the perfect kids, and the perfect house? No! You get to decide what *perfect* means to you. If your life does not work out how you planned it, it is okay. You can pick yourself up, dust yourself off, and move on to create a new plan.

Chapter 1
THE HAPPINESS

At the tender age of six, I met my best friend, Kirschna Linden. Our friendship was wonderful, and we never lost our connection. We called each other every day after school to check in on how the day went. We would chat on the phone for hours. My parents will scold me now as they find out why the telephone bill was so high. The landline was our only way of communicating because cell phones were not as prevalent as they are today.

We looked forward to the weekend because it meant that we could spend more time together. We would arrange sleepovers so we could catch up in person. My dad would take me to Kirschna's house on a

Friday and her mom would take me back home on a Sunday. What good times we had.

Time went by so quickly and before we knew it, we were getting ready for our final year of school. We both had extremely strict parents who ensured that we did not go clubbing before we reached this final year. We had a bit more leeway getting out of the house after high school.

When we started working, we would set money aside to take ourselves out. We would go dancing every Friday. We did not own cars at the time, but we always found a way to get to the club and back home safely. We would dance the night away without a care in the world. All we wanted was to dance, laugh, and be happy. Our Friday night clubbing culture led to me meeting the love of my life, my soulmate, the one that completed me and gave my life purpose.

One Friday, I went to Kirschna's house to get ready to go out, as usual. We tried to arrange transport for the night and had one disappointment after another. We wanted to give up on going out that night until one of her uncles stopped by. We asked him to drop us off at the club on his way home.

We got to the place called *Dominique's Paradise*. We bought drinks and found a good spot to settle in. As the night progressed, we hit the dance floor and danced in front of a huge wall-to-wall mirror. Kirschna and I were apart for a short moment as we danced, and as I turned away from the mirror to the view of everyone on the dance floor, there stood a guy that I had never seen before. He grabbed my hand and we just started jazzing (dancing). I know a lot of people; however, I had never seen this guy in Ennerdale before. Ennerdale is not a big place as almost everyone knows everyone. I knew Jacques, the guy that he was with, but I did not know him.

I danced with this guy and Kirschna danced with Jacques. After a few hours of a good dance session, Kirschna signalled that it was time for us to go. I whispered in his ear, "It's time for me to go. I love the way you dance." He was chuffed with himself and asked for my number. We all know about the number story. You stand and ask yourself, "should I give him the correct number? Do I want him to call me? Do I want to see him again?" All these questions swirl in your head as you ponder on the decision. I had an enjoyable time dancing with him and decided to give him the correct number. Thank God I did! He immediately dialled my number to ensure that it rang. He was impressed that I gave him the correct number and promised to call.

He called on a Sunday night. He was well-spoken, polite, and friendly. We spoke for almost an hour until it was time to say goodnight. He called again the next day and again we spoke for an hour. We had a natural connection and could speak about anything. The hour-long phone conversations carried on every night after work for the subsequent two weeks until he politely asked if he could visit me at home. Without any hesitation, I agreed to it.

I was shaking and my heart was racing as he called to let me know that he was outside.

I do not usually get nervous but somehow he made me extremely nervous. We greeted and sat on the front porch of my parents' house. We sat for almost four hours talking about our upbringing, our siblings, our friends, work – everything! I had a warm feeling of happiness.

We did not start dating for at least four months after our official meeting. It was not an easy four months, given how strict my parents were. I grew up in a house with both parents, Patricia and Lucas Nelson, and four sisters. There were four siblings from my dad's side that I did not grow up with. There were five girls in one house, and I was the youngest of the five. I was twenty years old at the time I met Hugh and he was twenty-one.

In those four months, we would go out with friends, go to the movies, or have dinner. We took long walks where we would speak for hours. When I finally introduced him to my parents, I introduced him as my friend. My dad would fight with me for coming into the house after 1:00 a.m. almost every weekend. He knew that I was out with Hugh. I knew I would get a scolding when I arrived home at that time, but I did not change my ways. I was happy when I was with him. He was simply different, and I enjoyed being around him.

One night my dad waited up for me. As I opened the door, my heart dropped so far down my chest as he sat there looking at me with rage in his eyes. He said, "Call that boy in here before he leaves." Hugh and I had a signal to indicate when I was safe in the house by flicking the outside light on and off. Instead of flicking it on and off, I switched it off and left it off. He knew there was something wrong and he stepped out of the car and walked towards the gate. As I walked back out, I gave him hand signals to show that we were in trouble. I told him that my dad wanted to see him. We got to the front door and my dad asked, "Hughy, do you think it is right to bring my daughter home in the morning hours?" He stood there with his arms folded and had nothing to say in response to my dad. My dad decided to ask a second question, "Do you think your mother would like it if your sister was brought home at this time of the morning every weekend by another woman's son?" He humbly responded with a tremble in his voice, "No Uncle Lucas, she would not." My dad then added, "If you want to see my daughter, come inside the house. It's not safe for you guys to sit outside after you arrive from wherever it is that you are coming from." "Yes, Uncle Lucas. Apologies Uncle Lucas. It won't happen again." My dad told him to park the car inside the yard and come into the house.

A few days later, he did as my dad had instructed. At that time, he had not gone further than the lounge. I asked him to assist me in carrying something from my room to the front door. He agreed, but the look on his face showed his nervousness. As we walked down the passage, he softly sang to me while stepping on each tile, "This is the furthest I've been in your house. This is the furthest I have been in your house. This is the furthest... This is the furthest..." He could not believe that he was truly in my room. As quickly as he got into the room was as quick as he got out as he was respectful towards my parents.

He asked for us to officially be a couple the day after my twenty-first birthday. He immediately said, "I would like to introduce you to my mom." He took me to meet his mom on the Sunday after my party. We parked outside and he asked, "Are you ready?"

We walked in and she was sitting in the lounge on a hot December afternoon. His mom and I both smiled as Hugh introduced us. She seemed like a nice person from the onset, and it looked like we would get along well. We made small talk for a bit and left. Since that day, his mom and I got on like a house on fire as we both had one thing in common: the love we shared for Hugh.

We announced ourselves as a couple to our friends. Everyone started cheering and clapping as we held hands and raised our joined hands in the air.

When we started dating, Hugh made sure to check on me from time to time during the day. We had date night once a week. He showered me with gifts on special occasions and ensured that he kept a smile on my face. That was when I felt true happiness.

We had a great relationship and a great friendship. Wherever we went, we would dance and be happy. He would always be on the dance floor with a circle of people around him. People would be chanting his name. He lit up a room instantly with all his sayings and jokes.

Hugh's reverse psychology on how to live life

One day I stopped and asked him, "How do you do it? How are you always so happy? How do you find it so easy to always laugh? You never get angry." That is when he explained his story to me.

Hugh Jason Jackson was born on 5 February 1985. He was the second eldest child after his late sister from his mom's side. He was the fourth child from his dad's side. He grew up with his mom and visited his dad during the school holidays. His dad lived in Zimbabwe for an exceptionally long time.

Hugh was diagnosed with type one diabetes at the age of nine and had to go onto insulin injections to manage his sugar levels. People with type one diabetes may require insulin when their meal plan, weight loss, exercise, and antidiabetic drugs do not achieve targeted blood glucose (sugar) levels. The body may require insulin injections to compensate for declining insulin production by the pancreas. As a young boy, he had to get used to this new way of surviving by eating a different way to his peers and cutting out sugar and fizzy drinks.

He felt like he was treated like an egg after he was diagnosed, especially by his dad. He got no more hidings and was no longer scolded because everyone was scared that something would happen to him concerning his condition. He always used to jokingly say his dad was so scared of hitting him after he was diagnosed as he thought the poor child would land up in a coma.

He further explained to me that he was a chubby child. I could not believe this until I saw the pictures. Weight gain is one of the biggest side effects of being a child diabetic as you develop an increased appetite, thirst, and excessive fatigue. He was often teased by his peers about being bigger than them. He dreaded going to school as he knew what the day had in store for him. This continued for many years even into high school, and he just allowed people to talk down on him and make fun of him. This affected his confidence as a child.

Growing up as a child diabetic affected his immune system due to all the insulin that he had to take. It led to some side effects which affected him in his adulthood. He had problems with his eyes and kidneys. There are eight complications[1] of childhood diabetes that one could experience: cardiovascular

---

1 Mayo Clinic. (2021). Type 1 Diabetes. Retrieved in July 2021 from, https://www.mayoclinic.org/diseases-conditions/type-1-diabetes/symptoms-causes/syc-20353011

disease; nerve damage, kidney damage; eye damage; foot damage; skin conditions; hearing impairment; and Alzheimer's disease.

If you have a child that suffers from this condition, you must have it treated and checked immediately and research the long-term effects that it brings along in the body.

He gained control over the weight issue late in his teenage years. When he got to college, he decided that he would not allow anyone to talk down on him again. He found his voice and chose to not give anyone the power to make him feel miserable. That was when he chose happiness. He decided that a day would not go by without him laughing and enjoying life. He realised that the dance floor cannot talk back, the mic cannot criticise, and the decks have no ulterior motives. He chose life. He chose to live each day as if it were his last, to love with all that he had, and to laugh because laughter is the best medicine for the soul.

He became more charming and confident as he got older. He had dark skin and would always challenge himself to go for lighter-skinned girls. His friends did not think he would ever get the girl, but he always did. The friends would stand in amazement as they tried to figure out how he managed to smooth talk these girls. Well, he just had that charm. When you speak to him you forget about everything and everyone else around you. It also helped that he was well-spoken as that would have you even more mesmerised. He had a unique voice and a contagious laugh.

When he decided to be this new Hugh, he became more outspoken, more active in meeting people and getting out there to do things. He entered modelling, dancing, and singing competitions. He even entered South African Idols. He decided that being happy was the only option for him following his childhood experience of bullying.

He had so much confidence and it was amazing to watch. We attended one of his year-end functions at work and the theme was pimps and you know what goes with a pimp. He went all out with his outfit and gathered items of clothing from family and friends to dress up as a particular pimp.

He wore a white pimp hat, white shirt, pink waistcoat, black flowing pants, black pointy shiny shoes, and a big bling chain. He wore the biggest and longest grey fur coat and had a pimp cane to top off his look. He walked into that venue with the highest confidence. He got several compliments throughout the night and even won the best-dressed award.

1 - Hugh Jackson in pimp suit

2 - Hugh Jackson in pimp suit

The master of ceremonies of the event could not make it and the manager had the program printed and laid it out over the mic to allow anyone in the auditorium to step up and be the master of the ceremony. Hugh had no hesitation in his mind as he bounced to the front (in true pimp style). The entire room laughed all night because of his ad-libs and jokes while hosting the event. We had a memorable event.

Proverbs 17:22 states that a cheerful heart is good medicine, but a crushed spirit dries up the bones.

Key Action

I urge you to choose happiness every day of your life. Choose to live happy because no one else can be happy on your behalf. You need to make a conscious decision every day to wake up and be happy.

Chapter 2
THE LOVE

I experienced true love for the first time on 5 February 2011—the day that he proposed to me.

The day was also Hugh's birthday. I had not planned anything for the morning of his birthday because he had gone to a funeral. Instead, I planned to take him out for dinner and present him with his gift.

He returned from the funeral earlier than I expected and had this smirk on his face that indicated that he was up to something. My hair was a mess, and I had no make-up or accessories on but had this rush of excitement when I saw him go down on one knee. I could see that he was sweating because he was nervous. He started, "Edna Nelson, I love you with all my heart and I can't imagine my life without you. Would you do me the honour of being my wife? Will you marry me?" I said "yes" without hesitation. I knew it was the right decision to make. We were meant to be together.

He was a God-fearing man who had a deep respect for me and everyone else around him. I knew I would have a good life with him, that he would take care of me, and that we would have a wonderful family. I knew that, after God, I would be his priority. I would not accept anything less than God first followed by us as a couple, our parents, our siblings, our extended family, and our friends.

We announced our engagement to our family and friends, and everyone was overjoyed. We had a meeting with our parents shortly thereafter and started the planning. We had two engagement parties: one with our close friends and another with our family and friends. We had the engagement blessed at Revival Centre Community Church where we attended and served under the ministry of the late Apostle Edwin Moodaley and our first lady Apostle Roda Moodaley.

Our spiritual parents stood in agreement with us in church. Our pastor and his wife Pastor Sebastian Daniels and Mrs Brenda Daniels walked alongside us from the time we joined their cell group. They took us as their children and opened their homes and hearts to us. They also introduced us to the most loving couple that counselled us before marriage—sister Eunice and brother Isaac. We had intense weekly sessions that helped us identify any issues that we needed to resolve. Planning a wedding can take a toll on a couple, but we saw it through.

Hugh reminded me that it was our wedding and I needed to be happy. He gave me free rein to plan everything from the invites to the table layout. All he needed to be concerned with was the playlist, the convoy of vehicles that would transport us, and his suit.

We were blessed to have our good friend, Joel Stols, manage the Birchwood hotel in the East of Johannesburg at the time we were planning our wedding. We met up with him one morning for breakfast and had a tour of the place. We both fell in love with it and decided that it would be our wedding venue. Joel introduced us to the events coordinator, Nathalia, who was amazing in planning our magical day.

We started planning on 16 June 2011 with the help of our parents. Nathalia gave us a confirmed wedding date of 21 April 2012. The date was set, and we were ready to get married.

Our wedding day arrived, and the house was abuzz with my mom, sisters, bridesmaids, and flower girls. We were up at 5:00 a.m. to get our hair and make-up done. We all looked immaculate, like models out of a magazine. We had our photographers and videographers from Gibson Photography capturing the behind-the-scenes moments while everyone was getting ready. I am often late, but on this day, I was on time and ready to meet my Mr at the altar.

The wedding was set to start at 1:00 p.m. and by noon we were ready to leave home—only to meet up with road works on the way. We only got married at 3:00 p.m. Hugh stood at the altar and had the patience that a groom needs to have while waiting for his bride. The moment we said, "I do" was magical and funny. Pastor Sebastian asked Hugh to repeat his answer as it was not loud enough and Hugh then shouted, "I DO!" and people burst into laughter. They all remember the big "I DO." We were married and we became one. We stood side by side with joy.

3 - The day Hugh and I got married

Our pastor explained to us that the woman belongs on the left-hand side of the man. She was made from the side of his rib to be a helper and not under his feet to be trampled on or under his fist to be beaten up, but right next to him as his equal, to assist him, to pray with him and for him. Proverbs 18:22 says, "He who finds a wife finds a good thing and obtains favour from the Lord." While Genesis 2:18 says The Lord God said, "It is not good for the man to be alone. I will make a helper suitable for him."

The best man, Ryan, taught us a unique way to toast. You would clink from the top of your glass and say, "Never above you"; then clink to the bottom of the glass and say, "Never beneath you"; and finally, clink at the centre of the glass and say, "Always beside you." Do not forget to make eye contact while you do this.

We had our first dance to Jennifer Hudson's *Giving Myself*. Just like when we first met, we danced the night away. Joel, Nathalia, and their team were so amazing and accommodating. They set up an extra four tables just before dinner was served as more people showed up. If you knew Hugh, you would understand why so many people wanted to share this special day with him. He was special and always said that you need to love yourself first before you can love someone else.

I will never forget the first experience I had with realising that you needed to love yourself. It was in 2002 when my dad got hijacked and shot. He was paralysed from the waist down. Our world was torn apart. He was hospitalised and rehabilitated for more than six months. We were called to the hospital for a counselling session so that we could be prepared for my dad's return home. The counsellor mentioned that my dad would no longer be able to use his legs. I remember just sitting there and zoning out. My hero, my pillar of strength, my lawyer, and my everything will not be able to do all the things he used to do as my dad. I sat there thinking that you need to love yourself enough to be able to face something so tragic. Many people would have opted for suicide after such news, but I knew my dad loved himself and his family too much to even consider such an act.

We recently celebrated his sixtieth birthday and I know now that it was his love for himself that carried him through those difficult days. It was by the grace of God that he was still alive. That inspired me to always love myself first before loving someone else. My parents always showed us the utmost love.

Make time to understand your love language and read Gary Chapman's book, *The 5 Love Languages*. In the book, he outlines the five ways that he believes humans show and want to be shown, love. These love languages include receiving gifts; quality time; words of affirmation; physical touch; and acts of service. Experts say that knowing your love language is imperative because it helps you understand the type of love you want to receive or the type of love you can give.

My love language is physical touch. I love to be shown affection and constantly need hugs and kisses from my partner. I feel neglected when I do not receive physical touch. You don't even have to say anything as long as you show me that you love me and that you are there for me, that is enough. Hugh's love language was quality time. We were both very social beings at the time and were at the peak of our twenties, however, we still had planned quality time on our date night every Tuesday.

Once you discover your partner's love language, it becomes easier to understand their likes and dislikes. This allows you to try and do more of what they like for the relationship to have more happy moments and happy memories.

Spend that quality time; buy gifts; give words of affirmation; physical touch; and acts of service. Do what you can while your partner is alive. This can be extended to your parents, siblings, and friends.

Key Action

Give love a chance no matter what. You never know if you might find your soul mate in that one. If you don't give love a chance, you might never experience the feeling of true love.

Chapter 3
THE HURT

The kind of hurt I experienced from the man I loved with all my being made me realise that life was short. You need to live each day as though it is your last.

I lost Hugh twice and experienced three sets of hurt in our relationship. The first hurt was when he broke up with me two years into our relationship. I thought everything was good and that we were at a stable point in our relationship, but I was wrong.

I would always go straight to his house to spend time with him after work before going home. We would sit and watch a few shows until the early hours of the morning—even on a weeknight. Weekends were even worse—we would only leave the room to make something to eat and to use the bathroom. Everyone around us would get so sick of us wanting to be in each other's arms the whole time.

One night I came back from work and went to his house, as usual. As I sat on the bed, ready to watch the next episode of Vampire Diaries, the Originals or Supernatural, he looked at me and looked away. I could see that something was bothering him. I asked what the matter was, and he said "Nothing," Before he could even switch on the PlayStation, he turned around and could not look me in the eyes and said, "We need to talk." I knew that nothing good ever comes after that statement, but I never expected the words that came out of his mouth. He turned to me and said, "I need a break from our relationship. I need a break from you." I asked if there was another woman and he denied it and continued to say that he needed a break. It did not make sense to me as I thought we were fine. It must be another woman. Again, he denied it.

After confirming one more time if there was another woman or anything that I had done, I decided to respect his wishes.

It was difficult to move on as we shared the same circle of friends. We worked together which meant that I would see him every day. How do I face him after this? Friends would beg me to come over and the first thing I would ask would be if Hughy was going to be there. I would decline the offer if I were told that he would be there. It was bad enough that I had to see him all day at work, I did not want to see him on my weekends out with friends. I discovered, a few weeks later, that there was another woman in his life. I kept thinking that it must have been the reason he broke up with me. How else could he have moved on so quickly?

I decided to move on too. There was a guy, Robert, at the club that always had a thing for me. I decided to give him a chance. It was more to get back at Hughy. That is when I knew what a rebound was—it was just getting with the next person because you were not over the other. There we were both in new relationships while having to face each other every day at work.

We used to go out with our group of friends to Soweto on a Thursday night for drinks and to catch up before the weekend rush began. We went out as my friends insisted that I could not break this ritual. They assured me that things would be okay, and they would make sure that a distance is kept between Hugh and me to prevent any confrontation.

When my family and friends greet each other, we always hug and kiss. I wanted the earth to swallow me when I looked at Hugh as I was not sure whether I should hug him or not. However, when I looked at his body language I decided to turn around and not hug him. Despite that awkwardness, it was a fun night out with friends.

When it was time to leave, Hugh's cousin, Chenaaz, asked me to drop her off at his house. I thought it was just a scam to get me to talk to Hugh because the awkwardness between us affected the entire circle of friends.

We got to the house and Hugh was standing outside with a few of his friends. I parked and said goodbye to Chenaaz. I decided to go into the house to get the rest of my stuff from him as I never wanted to set foot at his house ever again. He accompanied me to the room for me to pack all my stuff. While packing, we started speaking about the fact that we could not believe that we were no longer together and that we were both in new relationships. Everything was fine until he said that he felt like I did not fight for our relationship when he broke up with me. That's when I lost my cool and started shouting at him. "What did you want me to do? You are the one that broke up with me! What did you want me to do? I asked you repeatedly, why you needed a break and you kept on saying there was no one else but a few weeks after the breakup, I see another madam with a red car all over your Facebook!" I pinned him against the door and went on my knees asking him, "What did you want me to do? Did you want me to go down on my knees and beg you not to break up with me?" As he looked down at me, I retaliated with a smack from the bottom up to his face.

It turned into a screaming match as I accused him of cheating on me when all I wanted was to love him. He grabbed my hands and the drink that I had in my hand splashed all over the both of us, against the door and the walls in the room. While all the screaming and arguing went on, two of the friends he was with ran into the room and pulled us apart. I left and that was the end of it for me. I left in a state that night and went to cry myself to sleep—dreading to see him at work the next day.

Things carried on like this for another eight months between declining offers from friends, spending time with Robert and friends having to split themselves between Hugh and me.

Eight months later, he called and asked if he could visit me one night. I hesitantly agreed as I wanted to hear what he wanted to say. He came over and we spoke for hours, regarding what we had in our relationship and why it ended. Before the night ended, he asked if he could visit again and if we could go out for dinner someday. He was still in his relationship, but I was already out of mine. Someone had seen him stopping at my house and phoned his girlfriend. He wanted to leave so that he did not cause any trouble between the two of them. He told me that his heart was still with me, and he did not know why he ended it with me. He only realised after the breakup that I was the only person he wanted to be with.

A few weeks thereafter, he phoned again and said he needed to talk to me. He told me that I was the love of his life, his soul mate and that he only wanted to be with me. His girlfriend left him because she said she could not compete with us because she knew that he would always want to be with me. We decided to give the relationship another go.

After he proposed in February, four months after we re-united, we began with the wedding plans and house-hunting.

The Second Hurt

The second hurt came four months later. My monthly menstruation was late, so I decided to take a pregnancy test—it was positive. I called Hugh and said we needed to talk. He had started a new job and we had to wait until after work to see each other. I showed him the test and his eyes were filled with tears. "I'm going to be a father", he said. We were ecstatic. He hugged and kissed me and said that it was the happiest day of his life. We only told my sisters and close friends about the pregnancy. We went to the obstetrician-gynaecologist (OB-GYN) a week later, tested again and it was confirmed that we were expecting a baby. There was a little human growing inside of me, 2.5 months along. We were so excited about what was to come. We were engaged, getting married, getting ready to buy a house and now to complete our family, a little one was on the way.

One Sunday we had a family lunch at our home. Everyone kept on asking when we would break the news to the parents, but it was so nerve-wracking. I kept on asking him, and all he said was that we needed to wait for the right time. I spilt milk twice while the visit continued and broke a glass pot lid, and my eldest sister kept saying that we needed to tell the parents because that was a sign that something was brewing. Hugh just felt that the time was not right and that we needed to have a proper sit down with all the parents and tell them together. Both our parents had separated so getting them all together for a quick Sunday lunch was not easy.

A month later, I woke up feeling severe cramps around my abdomen and was bleeding. I called Hugh immediately and told him that I thought something was wrong and he needed to rush me to the hospital. We arrived at the hospital and had a few scans done by the nurses. They looked at each other and shook their heads. Not long thereafter, the OB-GYN came in and gave us the dreaded news—there was no longer a foetus in my womb. The pregnancy had miscarried. We were devastated about the loss of our unborn baby. I was sixteen weeks along.

I needed to prepare myself to be wheeled into theatre. The doctor explained that because I was so far along in my pregnancy, some remains from the foetus needed to be removed. They performed the procedure and when I woke up in the recovery room, Hugh was sitting next to me. The first thing he asked was if I was okay. I was a bit drowsy, and my throat was sore. All I wanted was to cry and sleep. He stayed with me until I was discharged.

It was agonising to realise that we had lost a child and would never get to know the person our little unborn baby would have become. We would never be able to picture what he or she would have looked like. We drove home and just comforted each other from the hurt that we had gone through. We had to find a way to deal with it and move on from that experience. God was with us all the way and that made it more bearable.

I realised that we all lose something at some point in our lives. It may be an unborn baby, a mother, a father, a partner, or other people we care about. We were brought to the earth to serve a purpose and once our purpose is fulfilled, we will die. It might have been the purpose of the unborn Angel to bring myself and Hugh closer together after our eight-month break-up. We all have a journey to complete on this earth and once our journey is complete, we need to go and fulfil our heavenly journey with our maker. We are borrowed to this earth because from dust we were made and to dust we will return.

The Third Hurt

A few months later, I experienced the third and final hurt. This loss hit the hardest because he was not there for me to smack him like after the break-up, or he was not there to hold my hand like after the miscarriage. This time I was on my own. It was final. He took his last breath on 25 April

2012 at 6:00 p.m. We would never hear that unique laugh of his. We would never hear him sing, see him dance, or watch him live his life as if it were the last.

Hugh had an incision made into his thigh to have the dialysis machine run through his body two weeks before the wedding. He needed to have dialysis done every second day for the rest of his life. In the last two months before he passed, his kidneys started failing and dialysis was the only way to keep him alive. The doctor explained that having the incision on the thigh was only temporary because he knew that our wedding was coming up in two weeks. If he had done the operation on the chest—the correct place to have it—Hugh would not have been medically fit to attend our wedding on 21 April. He would have needed at least three weeks to recover. He agreed to have the temporary operation done on his thigh and to go back for the operation on the chest after our wedding. Everything went well.

We had two more weeks to work on the final touches for the big day. We had our fairy-tale wedding, and it was everything we wanted and more. Our family and friends celebrated the magical day with us, and we danced the night away. On Sunday morning, we had breakfast with everyone that slept over at the venue. We opened gifts and counted money with family in the evening. Later that night Hugh said he was not feeling well. He woke up at 3:00 a.m. with extremely low blood sugar. His mom and I gave him apricot jam and coke to help him. He had had several low blood sugar episodes before, but this one was different. This one was incredibly intense, and he took longer to come to. While having the episode, he kept shouting that he was dying. His mom scolded him and said he should not say things like that. Eventually, he calmed down and we went back to sleep.

On Monday, I took him to the hospital to prepare for the operation he would have on Tuesday morning. On Tuesday morning, the matron of the ward came to tell him that the doctor had an emergency and that they would postpone the operation to Wednesday.

Little did we know that Tuesday night was our last night.

During the visiting hours, Hugh had several special visitors including close friends and family who showed up, namely Aunt Cynthia, Uncle Johnny, Joel, Jason, Jared, Thabang, Damian, Dominique, Chenaaz and me. We carried on like we owned the hospital even though he was placed in the Intensive Care Unit (ICU) where only two visitors were allowed at a time. We all sat around the bed, joked around, and watched a game of English football. One could not expect anything less from Mr Jackson -he was the life of the party even in ICU. We had a good visit with him as we were psyching him up for the operation the next day. When the game ended everyone left and I stayed another half an hour or so until the nurse came to tell me that visiting hours ended two and a half hours ago. I kissed Hugh goodnight and left.

The next day was the day of the operation. He was supposed to be wheeled in at 6:00

a.m. therefore, I decided that I would go for the 10:00 a.m. visiting hour. At 9:30 a.m. I called the ward to confirm whether he was out of the theatre and recovering. The nurse said that he did not go in for the operation but that it would only take place after 11:00 a.m. For some odd reason, I could not get out of bed. I was exhausted and I just wanted to sleep. I slept again and only woke up after 11:00 a.m. I phoned again to confirm whether he had gone in. The nurse then said he would only be going in at 1:00 p.m. At this point, even with my tiredness, I called his mother to let her know that Hugh would only be having the operation at 1:00 p.m. We decided to go to the hospital, accompanied by my mother and his aunt. We got to the hospital just after 1:00 p.m. and he had gone in for the operation.

We all sat in the waiting room ready for him to come out after an hour or so. An hour passed and he was not yet out. We tried not to panic and kept saying that everything was fine. Two hours passed and he was still not out. We started to get worried and went to one of the nurses to get information on why he was taking so long to come out. They needed to order blood because he lost a lot of blood during the operation and needed a transfusion. My mother works for the South African National Blood Services (SANBS) and when she heard that they ordered blood, she called the laboratory to confirm who was on duty and who would oversee getting the blood to the hospital. The person on the other end confirmed everything and said the blood would be leaving the lab in a few minutes. She made it clear that the blood was for her son-in-law. She instructed them to get the blood in transit and fly to Lenasia and emphasised that this was a life-or-death situation.

We started panicking three hours after the operation. My mom, his mom and his aunt said that we should join hands and start praying. We started praying in a circle asking God to keep his angels around Hugh and to keep him safe from any harm. At that point, we knew his life was in danger and all we could do was pray.

After the prayer, his mom was becoming extremely worried as she paced up and down the corridors. She was stressed by how long it was taking for the blood to arrive at the hospital. After a while, she disappeared. My mom went in search of her and found her close to the gate as she felt that she needed to go look for the van carrying the blood and that maybe they missed the turn. She was hysterical and could not fathom that we were about to lose Hugh. My mother had to calm her and walk back to the reception. As they walked into the front door, the blood arrived. We now had a bit of hope. They went back into the theatre.

An hour passed before they wheeled him into his ICU room. We had been waiting for this moment. Three nurses and a doctor surrounded him. Something was not right. He was moaning and groaning as they wheeled him past us. A few minutes later they said we could go in to see him. His mom and I went in to see him. As we walked in, I could see that he was in pain and did not want to talk. I just wanted to see if he was okay. "Hi babe," I said. He turned his head the other way and looked at his mom. He was still groaning, and his lips were very dry. I took my lip gloss and glazed his lips with that. I switched sides and he turned the other way, not wanting to face me. "Hughy!" I said and all he did was turn to the other side. We allowed my mom and his aunt to come in for a few minutes, and suddenly, the doctors and nurses asked us to excuse ourselves from the room.

We waited in anticipation. The anaesthetist came to us, and we were not ready to be told that Hugh was gone. We all ran into the room. There he laid on the bed, lifeless. All the jokes, laughter, talks, sarcasm, dancing, advice, opinions, everything out. He laid there unable to say a word. His soul was gone and there was nothing we could do to retrieve it. I walked toward him in disbelief, "Hughy? Baby", I said thinking that it was all a bad dream. I shook him a bit, but nothing. He was gone. After that moment all I could hear was a ringing noise in my ears.

Hurt People by Jussie Smollett is a song that helped me to understand hurt. It made me realise that no matter what you do, you cannot stop hurt and love. I was hurt and while I was going through the anger phase of my grieving process, my hurt made me hurt other people. I have included the lyrics below.

Hurt People
by Jussie Smollett[2]

"Broken-hearted people are the first ones
Once they've started, they can be the worst ones
Love is a weapon if you don't use it right
Now we are watching you come for my life
Hurt people hurt people
They don't know why
Hurt people hurt people
They don't even try, no
We all go through things in our lives
That don't make this s* all right
But you don't hear me

---

2 Smollet, J. (2018). Hurt People. Sum of My Music. Retrieved 8 July 2021, from https://www.musixmatch.com/lyrics/Jussie-Smollett/Hurt-People

Full Circle - How to Live, Love and Laugh

Listen clearly
Hurt people hurt people
Then they say goodbye
People hurt, people hurt, people hurt now
People hurt, people hurt, people hurt now
People hurt, people hurt, people hurt now
Then they say goodbye
Disrupted the vibe
Disrupted my life
Disrupted the tide, disrupt
Heartache, beating when you pull the fast ones
Lying, scheming
What kind of life is that one?
What would the world remember you for?
When love gets knocked down. It comes back for me
Hurt people hurt people
They don't know why (they don't know why)
Hurt people hurt people
They don't even try
We all go through things in our lives
That don't make this s* all right
You don't hear me
Listen clearly
Hurt people hurt people
Then they say goodbye
Hurt people hurt people

Edna Nelson

They don't know why
Hurt people hurt people
They don't even try
We all go through things in our lives
That don't make this s* all right
You don't hear me, no no
Listen clearly
Hurt people hurt people
They say goodbye
People hurt, people hurt, people hurt now
People hurt, people hurt, people hurt now
People hurt, people hurt, people hurt now
I ain't hurt no more"

Death be not proud is a poem that I used to read in school. I found it very intriguing and interesting even at that time. It was only after I lost someone close to me that it all made sense. We should know that death will die one day. After killing everyone, it would have no one else to kill and it will die. It should stop boasting about the number of people it kills because what would the use be to kill everyone and in the end it too would die.

Death be not proud
by John Donne[3]

"Death, be not proud, though some have called thee
Mighty and dreadful, for thou art not so;
For those whom thou think'st thou dost overthrow
Die not, poor Death, nor yet canst thou kill me.
From rest and sleep, which but thy pictures be,
Much pleasure; then from thee much more must flow,
And soonest our best men with thee do go,
Rest of their bones, and soul's delivery.
Thou art slave to fate, chance, kings, and desperate men,
And dost with poison, war, and sickness dwell,
And poppy or charms can make us sleep as well
And better then thy stroke; why swell'st thou then?

---

3 Donne, J. Death Be Not Proud. Retrieved July 2021, from https://www.poetryfoundation.org/poems/44107/holy-sonnets-death-be-not-proud

*One short sleep past, we wake eternally
And death shall be no more; Death,
thou shalt die."*

Hurt is something you don't have control over especially if it involves death. We will all face death at some point.

> **Key Action**
>
> Ask yourself, will I let the loss of a loved one get me down or will I let it lift me up and live how they would have wanted me to?

Chapter 4
THE FEAR

People tend to fear death because it is unknown.

I found myself sitting on the opposite end of the room as the ringing in my ears continued. I looked at Hugh in disbelief as he was lying lifeless on the bed.

His mom was crying, and she repeatedly called his name and tried to shake him as if to say, "Wake up." She was then sedated and taken to another room. I was also ushered to that room and found my pastor and cousin there. My pastor announced that the marriage had been registered. He received the news of Hugh's passing just a short while after our marriage, from **four** days prior, had registered. I could not comprehend that my husband had just died.

I went back to sit by his bedside and kept stroking his arm. He was starting to get cold. I sat there as people came to sympathise with me. I lost count of how many people came into the hospital room as they received the news of his passing.

The police and the mortician came to announce that it was time for them to remove his body and take it to the mortuary. "Two minutes more," I pleaded. That is when the ringing sound disappeared, and reality kicked in. My husband was dead and was going to be placed in the ice-cold fridge of a mortuary.

Again, they say, "We need to remove the body now". I heard the one guy saying, "He has a lot of fluids still secreting from his body and rigor mortis will start. We have to remove him and prepare the body for concealment." I turned around and said to the guy, "My husband just died, and you want to time me and be concerned about body fluids on the sheets. Is that your main concern?" I started screaming at him and said, "You can wait a few minutes more! I just want to say goodbye to him! Do you have to be in such a hurry?" That is when I broke down and started crying. I had been in a trance until then and could not express myself.

Ryan came and carried me to the waiting area. I sat there crying with my entire bridal party surrounding me with hugs and kisses. There was a bigger circle behind them including my mom, dad, sisters, cousins, friends, colleagues, neighbours, pastors, and our family doctor. There was no dry eye in sight. It was a sad moment in all our lives, and we just needed a moment to come to terms with what had happened.

They took him away in a black body bag. It felt like someone had ripped my heart out of my chest and drove over it with a BelAZ truck.

As I stood there, a voice said to me, "Do not fear death. He's gone to be with his maker and is gone to a better place." Psalms 27:1,

The Lord is my light and my salvation; Whom shall I fear? The Lord is the stronghold of my life; of whom shall I be afraid?

A lot of arrangements had to be made in the days leading up to the funeral. I was blessed to have a massive support structure that ensured that I never did anything alone. They assisted in making this heavy load just a bit lighter for me.

Our dearest friend Morwick Pietersen received the news of Hugh's passing the next morning because of the time difference between South Africa and the United States. He was devastated that he could not make the wedding and days later heard of his passing. He was all alone in a foreign country with no one who could understand the magnitude of what had transpired. He tried to video call and check in as much as he could to be supportive from the other side of the world.

One of Hugh's sisters, Betty, flew in from London the week before to attend the wedding. Luckily, she could make it and stay for the funeral. We had people drive in from other provinces to come to bid farewell to Hugh. This required us to delay his funeral by a week to wait for everyone to make it to Johannesburg.

He had a beautiful send-off coordinated by Ropers & Co. funeral directors. As we walked into the church, we were welcomed by a room full of mourners both inside and outside the auditorium. Everyone wanted to bid farewell to this wonderful man. A lot of people spoke highly of him. Everyone's tribute mentioned how they always laughed when they were around him.

4 - Hugh Jackson's memorial photo

He was buried at the Klipspruit Cemetery. He had a huge funeral, and everyone still could not believe he had passed on even after seeing him in his coffin. We had a send-off ceremony and then we released the homegoing doves and the coffin was ready to go down. That was the worst moment of my life—I felt like I could die. Seeing my newly wedded husband going down into the ground so soon after we said, "I DO!"

Our friend Joel had arranged for a special song as the coffin started its descent: Jennifer Hudson's *Giving Myself*—our wedding song. The song triggered everyone's tears as they remembered that just a few days before, we opened the dance floor with that song at our fairy-tale wedding.

From dust, we were made and to dust, we must return. Genesis 3:19 (King James Version), "In the sweat of thy face shalt thou eat bread, till thou return unto the ground; for out of it was thou taken for dust thou art, and unto dust shalt thou return."

Chenaaz, Hugh's cousin, continued to be by my side throughout that ordeal. If she could not be there during the day, she would make sure that she was there in the evening. She slept over most nights because she was worried that in my distress of losing Hughy, I would end up doing something to myself.

There was a night when she could not sleep over because she had other commitments. After having dinner, I decided to go and lie down on my bed and watch a bit of television. I felt that the television was too loud and switched it off. I turned on my side and closed my eyes for a bit. Just as I started drifting off, I felt someone getting into the bed next to me. I knew Chenaaz was not there. My heart started racing and my eyes almost popped out of my head as I felt the bed sinking in the shape of an adult. As I turned, I saw the shape next to me on the bed... There was no one there!

I knew it was him trying to connect— trying to tell me that he was there— trying to tell me that he wished he could physically be there to hold me and to tell me that everything will be all right.

A few weeks later, I went to bed as normal. On this night I was woken up by a chilly wind blowing in my face. I was frightened and turned around and checked the time—it was 3:00 a.m. My heart was racing. The next night again at 3:00 a.m., chilly wind woke me up. I told my mom about it. She smiled and responded that it must be Hughy and that I should speak to him when he comes again.

When it happened again, I would simply say, "Hi Jackson, you are starting with your jokes again." This carried on every night for three to four months, until it just stopped one night when I was getting used to it.

I went to read up on the number three. I found that the number is often associated with the holy trinity. Likewise, angel number three attempts to draw your attention to the spiritual world. It gives you information about your possible association with the spiritual world. Your connection to them is strong, and they can hear your desires and prayers. I think he was okay to let go when he saw that I was coping and regularly going to therapy. I was being weaned off the anti-depressants and sleeping tablets and was getting my faith back on track. I was slowly coming to terms with the fact that he was no longer there and all I had left were memories and pictures.

"To fear death, gentlemen, is no other than to think oneself wise when one is not, to think one knows what one does not know. No one knows whether death may not be the greatest of all blessings for a man, yet men fear it as if they knew that it is the greatest of evils."—Socrates.

Key Action

We do not know why we must be born just to die. We fear death but my encouragement is from a quote that has stuck with me and will remain with me for the rest of my time on this earth.

Chapter 5
THE ANGER

Everyone grieves differently and there are a lot of stages you can experience while grieving. These stages include denial, anger, bargaining, depression, and acceptance. One of the stages that I experienced was anger towards life itself. It was a terrible experience as it is not who I am. There was a time when I was extremely bitter and angry that I had to experience his passing so soon after we got married. I was angry at God, at the doctor, at Hugh, at myself, and towards the man on the street that did not know what I was angry about.

As I went through my therapy sessions, I realised that anger would not bring him back. He loved to see me smile. He loved to make me laugh and would have been upset with me walking around with all this anger. He would tell me to smile because it took more muscles for me to frown than it did to smile. He would tell me to find that thing that made me happy and use it to my advantage to conquer this anger—and I did just that. I love being around my family and friends—they are my HAPPY place.

For a long time after he passed, I would lock myself in my room and refuse to see anyone. I would put my phone off and refuse to speak to anyone. Once I switched it on, the first thing I would do is call his phone only to find his voicemail. I would dial his number repeatedly just to hear his voice. He sent me a voice note singing happy birthday during December before he passed away. That was my second comfort after the voicemail. I realised that it did not bring me any joy and instead, caused more anger. It took a while, but I decided to stop torturing myself like that.

I would take a drive and look at people. I would come across a man on the street who was focusing on his life, and I would ask myself what purpose that person served. What difference would he make in this world? I would ask God why He would leave this man to live and take Hugh that had so much to live for. He had so much potential and could make an enormous difference in so many people's lives. Why did he have to die? I felt like it was so unfair. I realised that it was unfair of me to think such thoughts. Who am I to decide that the man on the street does not have a purpose? God has a purpose for all of us. Hugh had fulfilled his purpose. He had done what God placed him on this earth to do. He ran his race, and it was God's will and He let his will be done.

I asked my therapist to schedule an anger management session for me. In that session, I discovered that I had not dealt with the reason I was angry. I was angry because he died. I did not want to be an angry person because people tend to associate anger with control. People feel like if they are angry, they can control everyone around them. They want people to tip-toe around them and it makes everyone else uncomfortable. People should earn respect and not want to gain control.

I went to the anger management class and the therapist started the session by asking me why I needed to speak to her on the day. I told her that I was walking around with all this anger inside of me and needed to get it all out. She asked me to go to the scene where the news was broken to me—the moment that he passed. She put me in a trance and played this ringing sound in my ear—the same type of ringing sound I heard at the hospital after he died. She made me explain to her repeatedly what happened. She made me deal with it and vent my anger. I had to repeat the hospital scene to her about ten times. She finally took the sound off and snapped me out of the trance. It was tiring and draining but it had to be done. I felt so good after that. I felt like I walked around with this burden for so long and once I dealt with it head-on, it made me feel lighter.

I realised that I needed to go through that ringing sound experience that placed me in that angry mode and finally brought me out of it. I am not saying that I immediately walked out of there and started laughing and smiling with everyone. It happened over time. I gradually changed my mindset, and said to myself, "Chin up and smile girl. You look better when you smile."

A kindergarten song just fits perfectly: Smile a while. We learnt from an early age not to be angry and not to fight, "Smile a while and give your face a rest. Laugh a while and ease your little chest."

Key Action

Take time to grieve the loss of a loved one. Go to therapy. I cannot stress enough how important therapy is. Go to therapy, get the necessary help you need to deal with the build-up anger after losing a loved one.

Chapter 6
THE DISBELIEF

Once the heart machine stops, there is no more life in that person.

We tend to think that we will live forever and that is why we go through a stage in our grieving called disbelief or denial. You cannot fathom that the person you love is gone. You feel like they might walk in at any moment and that someone was just playing a nasty prank on you.

After someone passes on, people always share details of their last words or how the person looked at them during their last encounter. They always end up regretting what they were told or what they saw then. Before Hugh passed away, he asked most of the mothers in his life to make soup and pork trotters. He phoned every day asking different aunts if they had made soup or trotters. Everyone kept saying, "No Hugh, not today, but when I make it, I will call you to come and pick it up." It was the last craving he had, and no one got around to making it. In the week leading up to his funeral, everyone kept on speaking about how they never fulfilled his last craving. His one aunt, Beauty, decided to prepare the meal for us to eat in his memory.

I have heard of a lot of people craving something before they pass on or people that say things in a puzzling way that leaves you wondering what they were on about. After they pass on, everyone reminisces on their last conversation and assert that the person said these puzzling things because they knew it was their last conversation. I do not know how true this is.

I always say that the reason that disbelief hits us so hard is that we cannot get used to death because it takes a different person every time. It is always someone that we least expect.

Take a moment to grieve. This will help you and allow the disbelief to slowly disappear. Allow yourself to heal. Do not rush grieving. It is not something that you can work through overnight—you must give it time. You must treat it as a wound, but one that is on the inside. You would need to wash it, plaster it, apply ointment, nurture it, and over time the new skin will start growing back. A scar may remain where the wound once was and that will constantly remind you of the hurt that you endured. Your heart is the same; allow the required time and go through the grieving process to heal it.

Stay on your knees and ask God to heal you. Go to church and receive the word of the Lord from your spiritual parents—this is like washing the wound. Go to therapy and speak about it. The therapist will take you on a journey that will allow you to deal with the grief—plastering the wound. Stay around family and friends as they will make you feel safe and make it easier to deal with the pain.

They will give you the love and comfort that you need during the challenging time—applying ointment. As time progresses, the loss gets easier to deal with as you allow the grieving process to take its course—nurturing it. Over time the heart heals and the pain of losing someone becomes a scar, but it heals, just as the wound heals. It will not be as bad as it was on the first day it happened. The pain you felt the first week after the fall or the loss takes time but eventually, it does heal.

I had to deal with being woken up at 3:00 a.m. and allow that part of the grieving process to see itself through. If I had dealt with it differently, it could have taken longer as that was a part of my grieving that I needed to deal with. The voicemail and voice note also helped me, but it took a while for me to watch our wedding video. That was the greatest gift. He left me such awesome memories that I will cherish in my heart forever. I am grateful for that because that was the last affirmation of how much he loved me.

Edna Nelson

Everyone said that our wedding day was his farewell. He was a wonderful person that had fun on the dance floor, despite having the pipe in his leg on the day. We laughed about so many things, and he lived like it genuinely was his last; and to top it all off, we all had a great time on the dance floor with him. The memories captured on film will last forever and that helped me in my process of dealing with losing him so soon after our epic day.

I had a conversation with my pastor, Sebastian, a few days before the funeral and he said to me, "My child, I am too young to be losing my children. You guys should be burying me and not the other way around." I replied with a smirk on my face and tears in my eyes, "What should I say pastor; Saturday morning I woke up a spinster; on Sunday morning I woke up a Mrs; and only four days later, I woke up and was a widow." In a space of five days, my title changed so many times and so drastically. It was unbelievable, to say the least.

The grief leaves you confused and in utter disbelief, but I promise you that with time comes healing and you will go through the disbelief phase that will leave you saying, "I wake to you everywhere, yet you are not here."—Nayyirah Whaeed

Key Action

Accept the support from family and friends. You will get through it—you just need to do the work. There is no way to go around it or over it, you have to go through the process to come out stronger on the other side.

Chapter 7
THE TRAUMA

Trauma will come but it does not last forever. As Psalm 30:5 states, weeping may endure for a night, but joy cometh in the morning.

Morning is a fresh start after the storm you faced the previous night. It is a second opportunity to see the sun rise and to realise that you can also rise above the trauma that you face.

No one ever wants anything traumatic to happen to them—it is too much to deal with. We prefer for life to be a bed of roses and do not want to be derailed because that is what trauma does. It takes you off course and your train wrecks and you need to rebuild the train to get back on the tracks. Rebuilding a train is not something that happens overnight. It could take months or even years. That is like losing someone you love. It is traumatic and it takes a while to recover from it. Some cultures make the widow dress in black and mourn for a full year.

Hugh's death taught me to prepare.

As humans, we need to prepare for the worst. The good Lord gave us a brain to think, plan, and prepare and to not be deceived by the dangling carrot in front of us. We need to prepare for failure, dark days, drought, rainy days, and remain alert in our lives. Plan for retirement, for your children's future or a headstart in life, or a family business to carry over for generations to come. Keep your policies up to date as the last thing you want when you die is to have people running around not being able to finalise anything because they do not have enough money to bury you. Keep a file with all your important documents such as bank account details, policies, funeral plans, and your will, amongst others.

I felt the trauma when the anaesthetist came to tell us that Hugh had passed, but Hugh made it easy for us as a family to deal with this as he kept all his policies up to date. There was no additional trauma with planning his homegoing. He was prepared and made it that much easier to prepare for his send-off. It gave me time to sit in silence in front of the Lord with my T.D. Jakes *Woman Thou Art Loosed! Bible*[4]. I read many scriptures that were relevant for a widow which gave me the strength to stand in front of an entire community and bury my husband.

Authoring this book came to me as a vision a day or two before his memorial service. It was destined to happen. I had so much time to sit in God's presence that He had time to lay this upon my heart. This was an instruction from the Most High, and on the day of his memorial service, I made it known to everyone that one day I would write about this great, wonderful man that lived and that it would reach the nation, the world, the universe. Everyone will know that

---

[4] Jakes, T. D. (2003). NKJV Woman, Thou Art Loosed Bible

there once was a man that walked this earth, and his name was Hugh Jason Jackson. He was my husband, my best friend, my confidant, and my soul mate.

"People think a soul mate is your perfect fit, and that's what everyone wants. But a true soul mate is a mirror, the person who shows you everything that is holding you back. The person who brings you to your attention so you can change your life. A true soul mate is probably the most important person you will ever meet because they tear down your walls and smack you awake. But to live with a soul mate forever? Nah. Too painful! Soul mates, they come into your life just to reveal another layer of yourself to you and then leave. A soul mate's purpose is to shake you up, tear apart your ego a little bit, show you your obstacles and addictions, break your heart open so new light can get in, make you so desperate and out of control that you have to transform your life..." Elizabeth Gilbert in Eat, Pray, Love.

Key Action

Deal with the trauma, face it head-on and you will come out stronger.

Are you going to let this trauma become a setback or a comeback?

Chapter 8
THE HEALING

God is a healer.

People believe that if something bad happens to them that God has forgotten about them somehow. Psalm 121:4 states that the Lord never sleeps nor slumbers. Since God never sleeps nor slumbers, there is no point in both of you staying awake. Go to bed and leave it to God!

God can never forget us; He is our maker and has a plan and purpose for every one of us—even though we forget him sometimes. We forget to pray, we forget to say thank you for the little things, and it is all those little things that build up and become big things. My mother always says, "We can plan but God steers, and He will steer your life in the direction that He had planned for you. Long before it even became a thought in your mind, He knew you before you were formed in your mother's womb." The scripture about planning that our Late Apostle E. Moodaley imprinted in our hearts was Jeremiah 29:11 which states, for I know the plans I have for you says the Lord, plans to prosper you and not to harm you.

Stay on your knees. Pray and seek the face of God. God is the main source of healing during a time of bereavement.

Go to church. When you go to church you can fellowship with other people and that helps a great deal as you are not alone. Getting the word from your pastor, breaking bread, and worshipping helps.

In addition to your biological parents, have spiritual parents. Your biological parents will always pray for you and with you, but you need to have spiritual parents as that is an additional prayer for you. The more prayers go up, the more blessings come down.

Have prayer warriors. You have your biological parents and spiritual parents who are all praying for you. Having a prayer warrior is an extra prayer. This is a person who is dedicated to praying for you every chance they get. This strengthens you ever more each day.

Go to therapy. Therapy is one of the key processes of healing. A lot of people do not believe in therapy, nor want to go to therapy, however, I would highly recommend it. It helps you deal with everything, and it allows you to put everything into perspective. It allows you to speak about everything and to work through it with someone that will pass no judgment and that is a trained professional.

I had been putting off watching the movie *Eat Pray Love* starring Julia Roberts. I finally sat down and watched it one Saturday with an incredibly good friend of mine, Mondre Bremner. Julia says something so profound at the beginning of the movie where she feels like she does not want to be with her husband any longer. She says that the only thing more impossible than staying was leaving. She did not know what to do and decided to pray.

After a painful divorce, she stood at the crossroads and decided to risk it all and embark on a journey of self-discovery. In her travels, she discovers the true pleasure of nourishment by eating in Italy, the power of prayer in India, and finally and unexpectedly, the inner peace and balance of true love in Bali.

There's a segment in the movie where she asks, "When does the grieving process end?" and her friend answers, "It will eventually end, but you have to do the work. You don't get a date on the calendar." Go to therapy, pray, get together with friends and family and work through every day. Once you are done and your day finally comes, you can love again, but you need to find the balance. "The balance is not letting anyone love you less than you love yourself." Once you find that balance you know you would never settle for less than what you are worth and truly deserve.

> **Key Action**
>
> Give it time. Healing takes time. Don't be too hard on yourself.

I just want to remind you to love yourself. Understand your love language. The next time you get an opportunity to raise a toast you can say, "Never above you. Never beneath you. Always beside you and cheers to love."

You need to make time to get closer to God. Book yourself a weekend away from the hustle and bustle of your everyday busy schedule and rest at God's feet. Give Him praise, give Him worship, and your healing will come. You must also believe it. No one can receive healing on your behalf. Someone can lay hands on you and anoint you day in and day out, but if you stand there in doubt, your healing will not manifest. Praise Him as you have never praised before.

One song that made me get up out of my chair in song and worship, the very next Sunday after Hughy's passing was *Still* by Hillsong. This song made me realise that no matter what storm you are facing, God is on the throne, and He will bring peace in any situation that you face.

Still
Hillsong[5]
Hide me now
Under your wings
Cover me
Within your mighty hand
When the oceans rise and thunders roar
I will soar with you above the storm
Father, you are kind over the flood
I will be still and know you are God
Find rest my soul
In Christ alone
Know his power
In quietness and trust
When the oceans rise and thunders roar
I will soar with you above the storm

---

5 Hillsong. (2003). Still. Hope. Lyrics retrieved August 2021 from https://www.azlyrics.com/lyrics/hillsonglive/still.html

Edna Nelson

Father, you are King over the flood
I will be still know you are God
When the oceans rise and thunders roar
I will soar with you above the storm
Father, you are King over the flood
And I will be still know You are God
You are my God
My God, my God, my God
Oh Lord
Find rest my soul
In Christ alone
Know His power
In quietness and trust
When the Oceans rise and thunders roar
I will soar with you above the storm
Oh, yes, I will
Father, You are King over the flood
I will be still know You are God
When the oceans rise and thunders roar
I will soar with you above the storm
Yes, I will. Yes, I will
Father, You are King over the flood
I will be still know You are God
When the oceans rise and thunders roar
I will soar with you above the storm
Father, You are King over the flood

I will be still know You are God
Oh, yes, You are
Oh, yes, You are
I will be still Lord

Another instrument I used during my healing was the New King James Version Holy Bible - T.D. Jakes *Woman Thou Art Loosed! Edition*. Hugh bought this for me as a Christmas gift the December before he passed. He also bought this for my mom and his aunt. He went out of his way to ensure we received it before Christmas day. It has special pink pages before every Bible verse and in his introduction, the bishop clearly states that he is excited about two things:

1. The mighty Word of God.
2. The powerful message of His healing and wholeness. Affirmation again that God is a healer, and His word confirms it repeatedly.

I found so many powerful messages while I went into my sacred place and poured my heart out in front of the Lord in prayer.

I will cherish it for as long as I *live*. I will use it the next time I need to *love* and as often as I can, to make me *laugh*.

The Lord is a healer, it is written in Psalm 147:3-5:

3. He heals the broken-hearted and binds up their wounds.
4. He counts the number of the stars; He calls them all by name.
5. Great is our Lord, and mighty in power; His understanding is infinite.

I am at a much better place in my life. I have a beautiful son named Bayden Leeuw, born on 15 June 2017. He was part of my complete healing as God blessed me with the most precious gift of life.

Nine years ago, I could take my time to sort myself out. I could take more than a year to go through depression and therapy and everything I needed to get myself to a point where I felt like I was normal again. After a failed relationship, I had to get up and move. I had to shake everything off and pull myself together because I had this little human who depended on me to see to him. I could not take a year or a month or even a week to decide if I should get out of bed. I had to take care of my son. I had to be his role model, and the best mother I could ever be.

I have found myself. I know who I am, and I am physically, emotionally, and spiritually mature. God knows why this is only happening now after everything that I have been through. I believe that it is the perfect timing—God's time!

I feel that my life has just come FULL CIRCLE!

ABOUT THE AUTHOR

My name is Edna Nelson, born in Grasmere (Ennerdale), the south of Johannesburg, South Africa.

I wrote this book as a commemoration of Hugh Jason Jackson. This book came to me as a vision. One morning I was half asleep and I saw myself writing the book. On the day of his memorial service, I shared my vision with the entire auditorium. I meant it when I said that the world should know that there once lived a man and his name was Hugh Jason Jackson, and he walked this earth with so much pride. I want everyone to know that you can live every day as if it is your last day on this earth. You can live loving everyone as though they were your flesh and blood. You can laugh too much. That is what I learned from him: a son, brother, cousin, friend, colleague, and Husband. I want people to know that you can have a life beyond a life-threatening illness; all you need to do is get up and do it every day of your life. You need to motivate yourself every day to do a little better than the previous day. Set goals for yourself and once you reach one goal, the next one seems as if it is at arm's reach. Do that every day. Have the drive to reach for the moon, and if you do not reach the moon at least you can get to the starts.

I also wrote the book to help people to deal with the loss of a loved one. I want to help everyone deal with loss better than I did. I want people to have the tools at their disposal immediately and not to wait four to five months before getting the necessary help that is needed. I want people to know that there is a God that is a healer. He has healed me and surely, He will heal you too. Go out there and live your life. Go out there and find the love of your life and if you are fortunate, you will find your soul mate just like I did. Go out there and laugh because life is too short not to laugh.

I currently live my life focused on five things: God first, my son, my family, my friends, and my job.

I work in the motor industry and run my events company on the side – Da Diva Girl Promotions.

I have just finished writing my first book and hope to write another one soon.

Ten years from now, I see myself at peace. I see myself having the "white picket fence" and having my children running around in the house and me not needing to worry about taking care of them in any way. Everything should be for them. I see myself as an established businesswoman and if I could, I would retire and spend every moment with my children and family. All I want is peace, love, happiness, and tranquillity.

I can be reached via the following platforms:

1. Email: ednanelson605@gmail.com
2. Facebook: Edna DaDiva Nelson
3. Instagram: nelson_edna
4. Twitter: Edna Nelson

You can reach out to me if you want to know more about my story.

I am always available for extra insight, private one on one sessions, group sessions or professional speaking engagements.

REFERENCES

Donne, J. (1633). *Death Be Not Proud*. Retrieved July 2021, from Poetry Foundation: https://www.poetryfoundation.org/poems/44107/holy-sonnets-death-be-not-proud

Hillsong (2003). Still. On *Hope*. Retrieved August 2021, from https://www.azlyrics.com/lyrics/hillsonglive/still.html

Jakes, T. D. (2003). *NKJV Woman, Thou Art Loosed Bible*. Thomas Nelson Incorporated.

Mayo Clinic. (2021, May). *Type 1 Diabetes*. Retrieved July 2021, from Mayo Clinic: https://www.mayoclinic.org/diseases-conditions/type-1-diabetes/symptoms-causes/syc-20353011

Washington, J., & Smollet, J. (2018). Hurt People [Recorded by J. Smollet]. On *Sum of My Music*. Retrieved July 8, 2021, from https://www.musixmatch.com/lyrics/Jussie-Smollett/Hurt-People

www.ingramcontent.com/pod-product-compliance
Lightning Source LLC
LaVergne TN
LVHW041229080426
835508LV00011B/1130